P9-AFZ-772

SPOTLIGHT ON SPACE SCIENCE

JOURNEY TO THE SUN

MAX KOEHLER

PowerKiDS press.

New York

Published in 2015 by The Rosen Publishing Group, Inc.
29 East 21st Street, New York, NY 10010

First Edition

Editor: Susan Meyer
Book Design: Kris Everson

Photo Credits: Cover (main), p. 7 NASA's Goddard Space Flight Center/SDO/S. Wiessinger; cover (small image of Sun) NASA/SDO/AIA; p. 5 © iStockphoto.com/Leonid tit; p. 8 NASA/ JPL-Caltech/Harvard-Smithsonian CfA; p. 9 NASA/JPL-Caltech/T. Pyle (SSC); p. 11 Digital Media Pro/ Shutterstock.com; p. 13 NASA/JPL-Caltech/R. Hurt (SSC); p. 15 © iStockphoto.com/Taily; pp. 17 (all), 18 NASA/SDO; p. 19 NASA/AIA/Goddard Space Flight Center; p. 21 © iStockphoto.com/Serg Aurora; p. 22 © Ruby Tuesday Books, Ltd./Shutterstock.com; p. 23 John R Foster/Getty Images; p. 25 Jamie Cooper/Getty Images; p. 26 Shutterstock.com; p. 27 © iStockphoto.com/James Brey; p. 29 NASA, ESA, C.R. O'Dell (Vanderbilt University), and M. Meixner, P. McCullough.

Library of Congress Cataloging-in-Publication Data

Koehler, Max.
Journey to the sun / by Max Koehler.
p. cm. — (Spotlight on space science)
Includes index.
ISBN 978-1-4994-0378-7 (pbk.)
ISBN 978-1-4994-0407-4 (6-pack)
ISBN 978-1-4994-0432-6 (library binding)
1. Sun — Juvenile literature. I. Title.
QB521.5 K644 2015
523.7—d23

Manufactured in the United States of America

CPSIA Compliance Information: Batch #CW15PK: For Further Information contact Rosen Publishing, New York, New York at 1-800-237-9932

CONTENTS

OUR SPECIAL STAR 4

ENORMOUS BALLS OF GAS 6

THE FORMATION OF THE SUN 8

THE PLANETS IN OUR SOLAR SYSTEM 10

WHAT IS THE SUN MADE OF? 12

FROM THE CORE TO THE CORONA 14

SPOTS ON THE SUN 16

RADIOACTIVE PHENOMENA 18

A VERY FAST WIND 20

GOING UNDERCOVER 22

BLOCKED BY THE MOON 24

FUELING LIFE 26

WHAT WILL HAPPEN TO THE SUN? 28

GLOSSARY 30

FOR MORE INFORMATION 31

INDEX 32

OUR SPECIAL STAR

CHAPTER 1

On a cloudless night, it's awe-inspiring to look up into the blackness of space and see thousands of bright, twinkling stars. It's easy to forget that there is one very special star that we see and even feel every day of our life. That star is the Sun.

About 93 million miles (150 million km) from Earth, this huge ball of burning gases creates a brilliant light in the blackness of space and forms the center of our **solar system**. It's impossible to tell from Earth, but the Sun measures about 870,000 miles (1.4 million km) across. That's as wide as 109 Earths set side by side.

It's easy to take the Sun for granted. It's always there, rising in the morning and setting in the evening. If there was no Sun, however, Earth would be a dark, frozen lump of rock. Without the Sun, there would be no life on Earth!

The Sun's heat and light are essential for life, from plants to insects to people. Our **planet** orbits the Sun at just the right distance. It is not too hot and not too cold.

ENORMOUS BALLS OF GAS

CHAPTER 2

For most of its life, every star in the universe is a massive ball of incredibly hot burning gas.

All stars live out their life in the same pattern. They are born. Then they enter the main part of their life when they burn gas for millions or billions of years. Then, as their supply of gas runs out, they die.

During the main part of their life, stars are made up of approximately 71 percent hydrogen gas, 27 percent helium gas, and about two percent of other **elements**. They are powered by a process called **nuclear fusion**. Inside the core, or center, of a star, hydrogen **atoms** are fused together, creating larger helium atoms. Nuclear fusion creates huge quantities of energy in the form of heat and light.

There are different types of stars. Red stars are the coolest stars, with surface temperatures

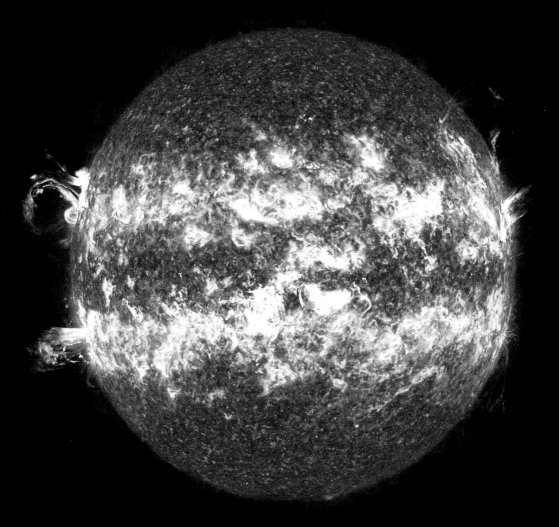

While our Sun is powerful, there are much larger and much hotter stars in other parts of our galaxy.

of about 4,500°F (2,500°C). Yellow stars, like the Sun, have a surface temperature of around 9,900°F (5,500°C). Sizzling blue-white stars reach temperatures of about 72,000°F (40,000°C).

THE FORMATION OF THE SUN

CHAPTER 3

About 5 billion years ago, the chemical ingredients for the Sun and everything in the solar system—including you—were floating in a beautiful cloud of gas and dust called a **nebula**.

Then, part of the cloud began to collapse on itself. Gas and dust collected, creating a massive sphere, or ball. As the sphere rotated in space, a disk formed around the sphere from the remaining

This hazy nebula is called Rho Ophiuchi. Its center contains about 300 superhot, newborn stars.

This artwork shows the birth of a solar system. A new star sits in the center. The surrounding dust is slowly forming planets.

gas and dust. Pressure built up as the material in the sphere was pressed together by **gravity**, causing the sphere's core to heat up and reach temperatures of around 18,000,000°F (10,000,000°C). Finally, the sphere ignited, and the Sun was born!

Inside the spinning disk, leftover matter from the formation of the Sun clumped together. This matter formed Earth, the other planets, their moons, and other objects in our solar system.

THE PLANETS IN OUR SOLAR SYSTEM

CHAPTER 4

Our solar system is made up of the Sun, eight planets, including Earth, and **dwarf planets**, such as Pluto and Sedna. The solar system also includes the planets' moons and objects such as **asteroids** and **comets**.

If you added up the **mass** of all the planets, dwarf planets, moons, and other objects in the solar system, their total mass would only add up to 0.5 percent of the entire mass of the solar system. The mass of the Sun accounts for the other 99.5 percent!

The Sun is so massive that its gravity pulls everything in the solar system toward it. That's why every object in the solar system continually orbits, or moves around, the Sun. Nothing can escape the gravitational pull of our huge star.

Moving away from the Sun, the eight planets of our solar system are Mercury, Venus, Earth, Mars, Jupiter, Saturn, Uranus, and Neptune. In this image, the planets' sizes and distances from each other are not to scale.

The solar system is also in orbit around the center of the Milky Way galaxy. Even though the solar system is moving through space at 157 miles per second (252 km/s), it takes between 225 and 250 million years to complete one orbit.

WHAT IS THE SUN MADE OF?

CHAPTER 5

Like all stars, the Sun is made up of hydrogen and helium. It also contains a small quantity of other elements, including oxygen, carbon, and nitrogen.

The gases and other materials that make up the Sun form a kind of matter called plasma. Plasma is superheated matter that has become so hot that its atoms have lost some of or all their **electrons**.

Inside the huge, boiling mass of plasma that is the Sun, over 660 million tons (600 million mt) of hydrogen are fused together every second to form 657 million tons (596 million mt) of helium. The missing tons (mt) are converted into energy.

It's impossible to imagine that quantity of energy, but here's one way to look at it. Take the amount of energy used in the United States in one year, multiply it by 1 million, and that's how much energy the Sun produces every second!

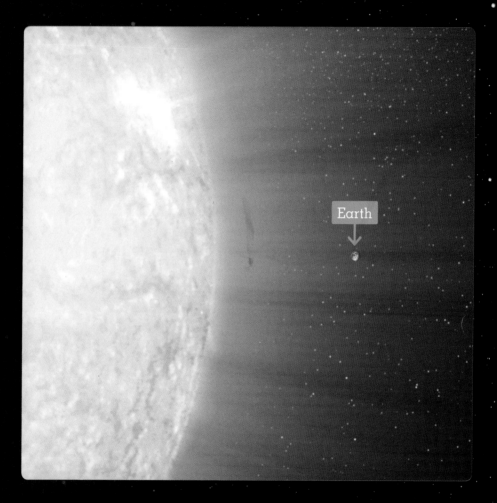

This artwork shows the immense size of the Sun compared to our planet. Earth does not actually orbit this close to the Sun. If it did, it would be burned to a crisp!

FROM THE CORE TO THE CORONA

CHAPTER 6

About 99 percent of the energy generated by the Sun through nuclear fusion is produced in its core. In the Sun's core, temperatures reach 27,000,000°F (15,000,000°C). Here, the plasma is about 150 times denser than water.

Energy generated in the Sun's core is transported by photons. These high-energy particles travel out through the Sun's radiation zone and convection zone to the Sun's surface, or photosphere. From the photosphere, energy generated in the core streams into the Sun's **atmosphere** and out into space. It's this energy that lights and heats our planet.

The movement of photons from the Sun's core to its surface is not instant. In fact, it can take around 150,000 years for energy to reach the photosphere. This means the light from the Sun that you see today was produced when humans were still living in the Stone Age!

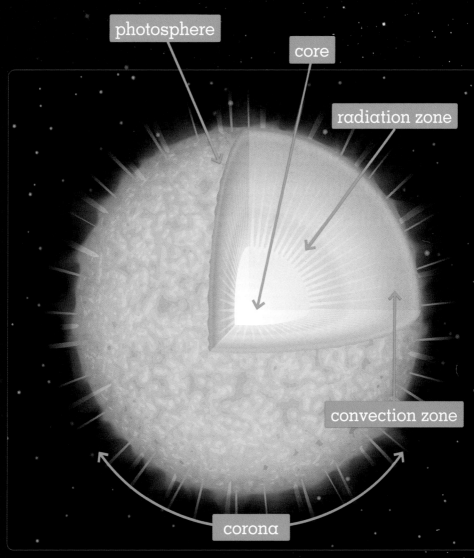

photosphere

core

radiation zone

convection zone

corona

This diagram shows the Sun's layers. The corona is the Sun's outer atmosphere.

SPOTS ON THE SUN

Among the **phenomena** that **astronomers** study on the Sun are sunspots. Sunspots look like dark blotches on the Sun's bright surface. They are caused by magnetic activity blocking the flow of heat from inside the Sun to its surface. Sunspots look dark because they are cooler than the area around them.

Sunspots can be as large as 50,000 miles (80,000 km) in diameter. As they move over the Sun's surface, they expand and contract.

Scientists have discovered that activity on the Sun follows an 11-year cycle. During periods of high activity, hundreds of sunspots may be visible on the Sun in a day. Clouds of plasma and gas may also explode from the Sun's surface. These periods in time are known as the solar maximum. During years of low activity, known as the solar minimum, the Sun may go for days with little or no activity and no sunspots visible.

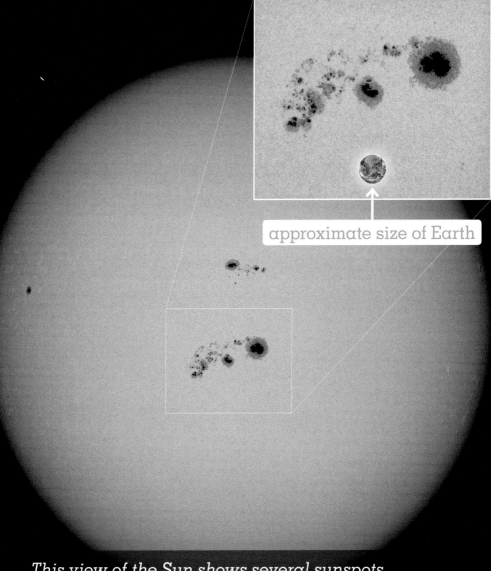

approximate size of Earth

This view of the Sun shows several sunspots.
Sunspots are often much wider than Earth itself!

RADIOACTIVE PHENOMENA

CHAPTER 8

In addition to sunspots, beautiful phenomena called solar flares and solar prominences also occur on the Sun. A person should never look directly at the Sun because it will seriously damage their eyes. Astronomers only view the Sun through special telescopes that allow them to view the Sun safely on a computer screen.

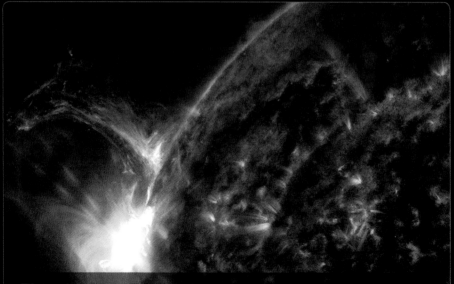

This solar flare was photographed by NASA's Solar Dynamics Observatory (SDO) in 2014. The SDO is a satellite that is studying the Sun.

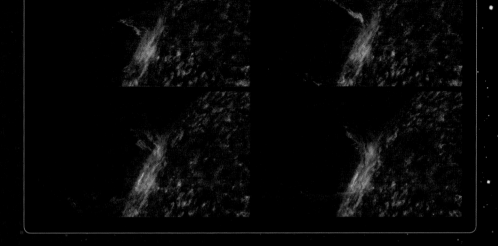

The glowing loop of a solar prominence may extend for hundreds of thousands of miles (km) out into space.

A solar flare is a large burst of radiation from the Sun's surface. Solar flares may last for hours or for just a few minutes. These intensely bright phenomena look like explosions on the Sun.

A solar prominence is a massive, glowing loop of plasma that bursts out into the corona. Prominences are anchored, or connected, to the Sun in the photosphere. A prominence usually appears in just a single day, but it may last for several months.

A VERY FAST WIND

In addition to heat and light, the Sun also gives off a steady stream of particles known as the solar wind.

These particles are pieces of atoms that have become free from one another because of the intense heat of the Sun. The solar wind rushes out from the Sun in every direction at an average speed of 250 miles per second (400 km/s). Traveling this fast, the solar wind can complete the 93-million-mile (150 million km) journey to Earth in just four days.

The solar wind spreads out from the Sun, creating a kind of bubble that surrounds the solar system. This bubble is known as the heliosphere. When the solar wind reaches the outer edge of the solar system, it mixes with winds from other stars in the Milky Way.

When the solar wind collides with Earth's atmosphere, it creates a beautiful glow called an aurora. Auroras may look like rays, streamers, or curtains of colorful light in the sky.

GOING UNDERCOVER

Perhaps the most fascinating solar phenomena are solar eclipses. During a partial eclipse, a section of the Sun is covered by the Moon. During a total eclipse, however, the entire Sun disappears, and day turns to night. So what causes these incredible events to happen?

For billions of years, the Moon has been orbiting Earth, and together, the Moon and Earth have been orbiting the Sun. This relationship between Earth, the Moon, and the Sun makes it possible for eclipses to happen.

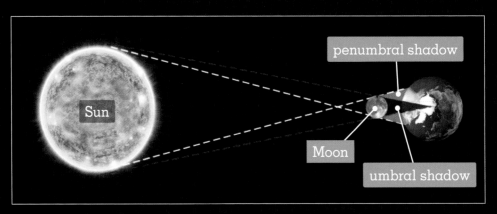

This diagram shows the Moon's shadows. The diagram is viewed from above and is not to scale.

In a partial eclipse, a portion of the Sun is still visible. This portion is dangerously bright, so be careful to never stare directly at a solar eclipse!

When the Moon passes between the Sun and Earth, it creates two shadows. These are known as a penumbral shadow and an umbral shadow. Most of the time, these shadows miss the Earth. Sometimes, however, the orbits of Earth and the Moon are in just the right position, and the Moon's penumbral shadow falls on Earth. Then a partial eclipse happens. From the part of the world where the penumbral shadow falls, it's possible to see the Moon's dark disk cover part of the Sun.

BLOCKED BY THE MOON

CHAPTER 11

Sometimes, when the orbits of the Moon, Earth, and the Sun are just right, the Moon passes directly between Earth and the Sun.

During a total eclipse, the Moon's umbral shadow falls on just a small section of Earth. From this area, it's possible to see the Moon completely block out the Sun, turning day to night for just a few minutes.

The math that makes total eclipses possible is amazing. The Moon is 400 times smaller than the Sun. The distance between Earth and the Sun, however, is 400 times greater than the distance between Earth and the Moon. This matching up of size and distance makes the Moon exactly the right size to completely eclipse the Sun.

A total eclipse happens somewhere on Earth about once every two years. As the Moon moves

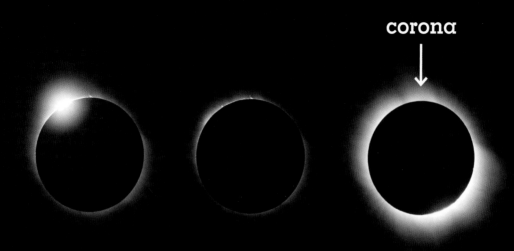

corona

The Sun's corona is not normally visible. As the Sun disappears behind the Moon during a total solar eclipse, however, the beautiful corona appears.

precisely into place to block out the Sun's light, stars appear, birds become quiet and stop flying, and animals get ready to go to sleep. The temperature may also drop by up to 60°F (16°C).

25

FUELING LIFE

CHAPTER 12

As a star, the Sun is not particularly special, and it has no unusual features. Like the estimated 1 to 4 billion or so other stars in the Milky Way, it is just a ball of burning gas. To every living thing on Earth, however, the Sun is essential.

One very important way that the Sun makes life on Earth possible is by providing us with food. Without sunlight, we would have nothing to eat!

Plants survive by making their own food. They take in water from the soil and carbon dioxide from the air. Then inside their leaves, they use sunlight to turn these ingredients into the energy they need to live and grow. This process is called photosynthesis. Without sunlight, plants could not exist, and

Plants are food for humans and other animals.

Plants, as well as algae such as seaweed, rely on sunlight to perform photosynthesis.

without plants, humans and other animals would have nothing to eat. Even carnivorous animals need plants, because plant life feeds the prey that meat eaters feed on.

Sunlight makes life on Earth possible in another way, too. During photosynthesis, plants give off oxygen from their leaves. Without oxygen to breathe, no animals could survive on Earth.

WHAT WILL HAPPEN TO THE SUN?

CHAPTER 13

Stars like our Sun may live for billions of years. Eventually, however, their supply of hydrogen fuel burns out. Then their life comes to an end. This will happen to our Sun in around 5 billion years.

As the Sun's fuel runs out, it will swell in size to become a red giant star. Its diameter will increase by up to 250 times. As it swells, it will swallow up Mercury and then Venus. Eventually Earth will come to a fiery end as it is engulfed by the Sun. After about a billion years, the Sun will begin to expel, or blow off, its outer layers. These layers of gas and dust will form a cloud, known as a planetary nebula. Finally, the remains of the Sun's core will collapse, leaving just a small, dense object called a white dwarf.

Where our Sun once burned, a beautiful nebula will be floating in the Milky Way. The Sun, our

28

Earth, and everything on Earth, will have become a cloud of ingredients with the potential to one day become new stars and possibly new worlds.

This is the Helix Nebula, one of the closest planetary nebulae to Earth.

GLOSSARY

asteroid: A small, rocky body in space.

astronomer: A person who studies stars, planets, and other objects in outer space.

atmosphere: The gases that surround a planet or star.

atom: The smallest particle of a substance that can exist by itself.

comet: An object in outer space that consists primarily of ice and dust, and that often develops one or more long tails when near the Sun.

dwarf planet: A body in space that orbits the Sun and is shaped like a sphere but is not large enough to clear other planets from its orbit.

electron: A very small particle of matter that has a negative electrical charge.

element: One of the basic substances that are made of only one kind of atom.

gravity: The natural force that causes planets and stars to move towards each other.

mass: A measure of how much matter something has.

nebula: A cloud of gas and dust in outer space, visible in the night sky either as a bright patch or as a dark patch against other luminous matter.

nuclear fusion: An atomic reaction in which two or more nuclei join together to form a larger nucleus, releasing huge amounts of energy in the process.

phenomenon: Something that can be observed and studied and that typically is unusual or difficult to understand or explain fully. The plural is phenomena.

planet: A large, round object in space that travels around a star.

solar system: The Sun, planets, moons, and other space objects.

FOR MORE INFORMATION

BOOKS

Gregoire, Maryellen. *Our Sun*. North Mankato, MN: Capstone Press, 2012.

Heos, Bridget. *What Is the Sun?*. New York, NY: Rosen Publishing Group, 2014.

Portman, Michael. *What Is an Eclipse?* New York, NY: Gareth Stevens Publishing, 2014.

WEBSITES

INDEX

A
atmosphere, 14, 15, 21
aurora, 21

C
convection zone, 14, 15
core, 6, 9, 14, 15, 28
corona, 15, 19, 25

D
dust, 8, 9, 28

E
energy, 6, 12, 14, 26

G
gas, 4, 6, 8, 9, 12, 16, 26, 28
gravity, 9, 10

H
heat, 5, 6, 14, 16, 20
heliosphere, 20
helium, 6, 12
hydrogen, 6, 12, 28

L
light, 4, 5, 6, 14, 20, 21, 25

N
nebula, 8
nuclear fusion, 6, 14

P
partial eclipse, 22, 23
penumbral shadow, 22, 23
photons, 14
photosphere, 14, 15, 19
photosynthesis, 26, 27
planetary nebula, 28, 29
plasma, 12, 14, 16, 19

R
radiation zone, 14, 15
red giant, 28

S
shadows, 22, 23
solar eclipses, 22, 23, 25
solar flares, 18, 19
solar maximum, 16
solar minimum, 16
solar prominences, 18, 19
solar system, 4, 8, 9, 10, 11, 20
solar wind, 20, 21
sunspots, 16, 17, 18

T
total eclipse, 22, 24, 25

U
umbral shadow, 22, 23, 24

W
white dwarf, 28